UNCOVERING AMERICAN HISTORY™

A Primary Source Investigation of The Continental Congress

Xina M. Uhl and Betty Burnett, PhD

rosen publishing's rosen central
New York

Published in 2019 by The Rosen Publishing Group, Inc.
29 East 21st Street, New York, NY 10010

First Edition

Library of Congress Cataloging-in-Publication Data

Names: Uhl, Xina M., author. | Burnett, Betty, 1940– author.
Title: A primary source investigation of the Continental Congress / Xina M. Uhl and Betty Burnett, Ph.D.
Description: New York : Rosen Central, 2019 | Series: Uncovering american history | Includes bibliographical references and index. | Audience: Grades 5–8.
Identifiers: LCCN 2018008326| ISBN 9781508184126 (library bound) | ISBN 9781508184119 (pbk.)
Subjects: LCSH: United States. Continental Congress—Juvenile literature. | United States—Politics and government—1775–1783—Juvenile literature. | United States—Politics and government—1783–1789—Juvenile literature. | CYAC: United States. Continental Congress—Sources. | United States—Politics and government—1775–1783—Sources. | United States—Politics and government—1783–1789–Sources.
Classification: LCC E303 .B89 2019. | DDC 973.3/12—dc23
LC record available at https://lccn.loc.gov/2018008326

Manufactured in the United States of America

On the cover: This oil painting, called *The Declaration of Independence, 1776,* is by Allyn Cox. It depicts five delegates to the Second Continental Congress: (*left to right*) Benjamin Franklin, Roger Sherman, Thomas Jefferson, Robert Livingston, and John Adams.

CONTENTS

INTRODUCTION

The first permanent settlement in North America by English colonists began at Jamestown on May 14, 1607. Prior to this time, the Spanish had dominated settlement in North America. This effort by the English brought a new era to the New World.

Though the first English settlers struggled with high death rates due to disease and starvation, they persevered. Over the next century and a half, British subjects from Scotland, Ireland, Wales, and England flooded to America and set up thirteen colonies. Scattered among them were French, German, and Dutch settlements. African slaves and Native Americans joined those of European origin.

Three main groups made up the colonies. The first group, New England, lay along the North Atlantic coast. It included Massachusetts, Connecticut, New Hampshire, the territory of Vermont, and Rhode Island. The people were mostly merchants, farmers, craftspeople, and seafarers with strong ties to church and community and a thriving interest in local government. Their major port and largest city was Boston.

The second group was called the middle colonies. It included Maryland, New York, New

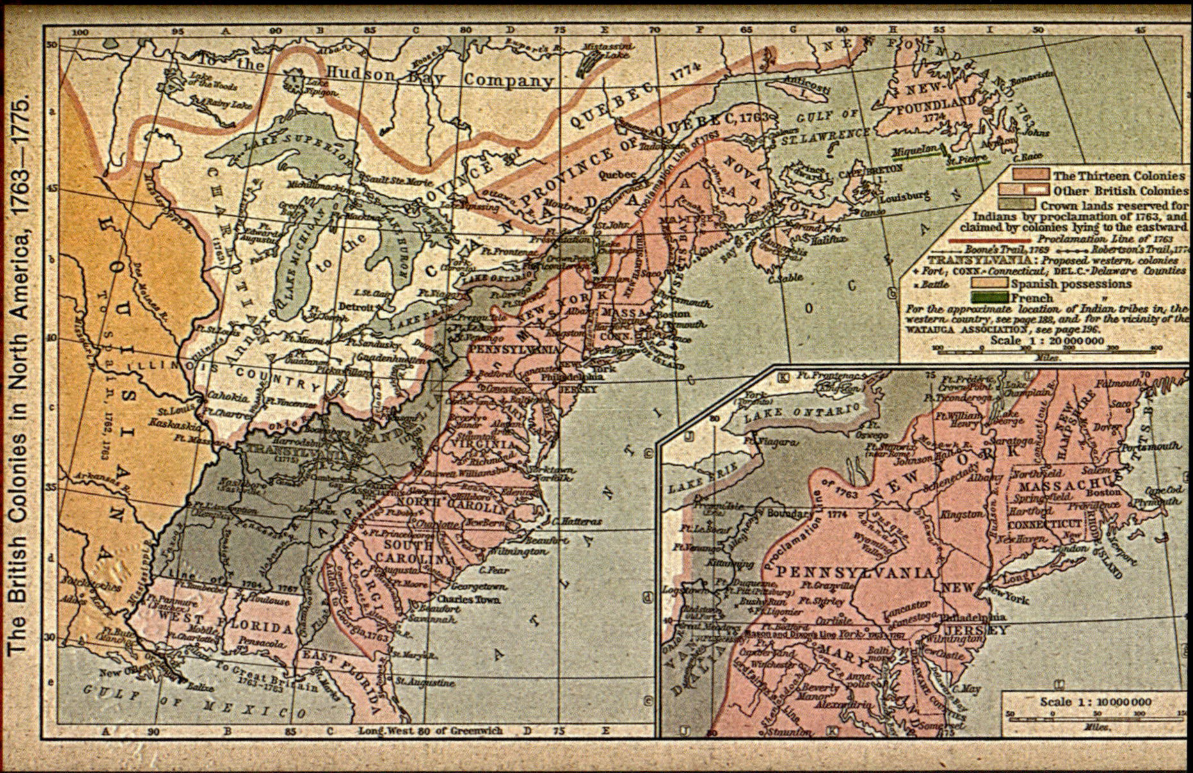

This map shows the thirteen original colonies as they stood from 1763 until 1775. All were founded by the British except New York, by the Dutch, and Delaware, by the Swedish.

Jersey, Delaware, and Pennsylvania. Philadelphia was the largest city there. It was known for its religious diversity, which included twelve different religious denominations. The Dutch founded New York City, where many varieties of Europeans and free Africans settled.

The third group of colonies were the southern ones. They included Virginia, the Carolinas, and Georgia. Though sparsely populated, the great rice and tobacco plantations along the rivers made it a prosperous area. The largest city was well known as a hub of English culture—the port town of Charleston, South Carolina.

Most English settlers came to America for economic opportunities, though some came mainly because they wanted the freedom to practice their religion as they pleased. The settlers valued education. If citizens could read, write, and think for themselves, they reasoned, then they became worthy participants in government. In most of Europe, only the very wealthy were educated, and the nobility controlled local government.

Women, Native Americans, and African Americans were not allowed to participate in government, though. Only white male property owners could vote or seek office. In some colonies, voters also had to be members of the accepted Protestant church.

English settlers brought with them two important political ideas. The first was that people can create their own governments, and the second was that people have a right to govern themselves. Settlers in Spanish or French colonies did not question the right of kings to make unpopular laws, and they did not have a tradition of voting for public officials. All the English colonies had legislatures (governing bodies responsible for passing and enforcing laws). Some legislators were elected; others were appointed.

Despite their differences, a shared language and history linked the thirteen colonies. Royal charters had established each colony, but some were managed and owned by businesses and known as proprietary colonies, while others were royal colonies run by a governor the king appointed. Some colonies in New England had self-government from the beginning. By the late eighteenth century, the population of the colonies exceeded two million.

Ties to England remained strong, and each colony was its own separate area, not united with the others. This worked well while the monarchs did not interfere in the colonists' lives and Parliament, England's governing body, treated them with the fairness they believed they deserved. But in 1763, that began to change in a series of events that would lead to the formation of a new nation.

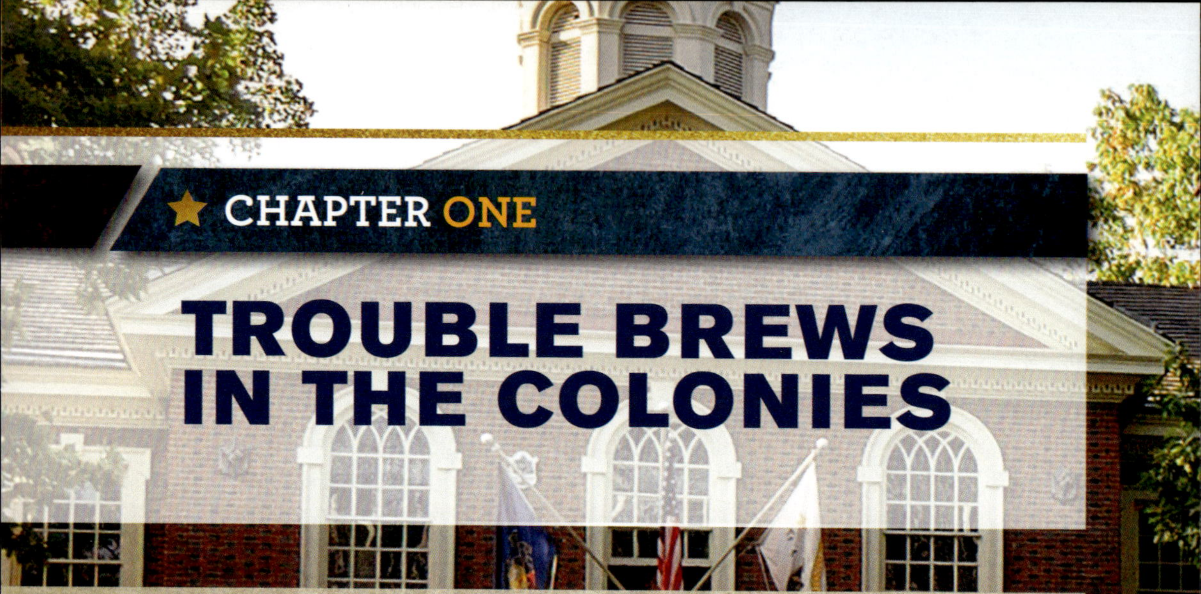

★ CHAPTER ONE

TROUBLE BREWS IN THE COLONIES

Since the establishment of the Jamestown settlement in 1607, the American colonies had maintained a state of peace with their rulers in Great Britain. But in 1763, a combination of economic and political reasons brought the two countries to the brink of war.

PROFIT AND LOSS

From England's point of view, its relationship with the colonies was an economic one. Colonies were an essential part of England's mercantile system. Under mercantilism, colonies were established for one reason: to serve the mother country. The American colonies supplied raw material, such as lumber, to England for manufacture there, and they were a market for English-made goods. By law, the colonies were not allowed to manufacture goods that could be made in England, and they could buy only English-made goods. Colonial business owners were not allowed to trade with other countries on their own. American crops, especially tobacco, rice, and

This illustration portrays some of the work that went on in the colonies: chopping, packing, milling, and plowing fields. In the background, ships leave the port full of goods to sell to other countries.

indigo, could be exported only to England or to another English colony. These laws limited America's growth.

Trade—exporting and importing goods—was the major source of revenue for the American colonies, and their welfare depended on it. The port cities of Boston and Charleston were full of activity, with ships arriving weekly to be unloaded and loaded. England regulated trade with all of its colonies in Asia and Africa, as well as in

America, through the Navigation Acts. One law specified that goods imported or exported by English colonies had to be shipped on English-made ships by English crews. ("English" included Americans.) By 1760, nearly half of the English ships were American-built, and shipbuilding was a profitable industry.

Mercantilism was considered a good system because it ensured markets for both England and its colonies, but it did not allow the colonies to expand independently of the mother country.

Boston Tea Party, by W. D. Cooper, depicts American colonists in Boston throwing tea cargo off British ships, which they did to protest a tax imposed on tea by Britain.

INTERNATIONAL ENEMIES

The American colonies and Great Britain were separated by the Atlantic Ocean. Communication between the two was very slow because it took several weeks to cross the Atlantic by ship. It was easy for years to go by without conflict. As long as trade was profitable, the English Parliament was not concerned about what English subjects in the colonies were doing.

French colonists were another matter. From the beginning years of English settlement, France and England fought for control of the North American continent. In 1754, a war began between the French and their Indian allies, and the English. In 1763, France surrendered, and England took over Canada and the West Indies.

The French and Indian War was expensive. The English Parliament decided to pay its bills by taxing the colonies. It also decided to keep ten thousand British troops, called redcoats, in the colonies to make certain that the French did not return. Both decisions were very unpopular in America.

For the next ten years, a series of tax acts infuriated the colonists, who saw no reason to pay England's debts when they had had no say about them. "Taxation without representation is tyranny!" they shouted. They felt they were being ruled by a cruel dictatorship. When they refused to pay the taxes or boycotted (refused to buy) English products, Parliament reacted by passing even harsher laws to punish the rebels.

Beginning in the 1770s, the ideas of a few men—Samuel Adams, James Otis, John Dickinson, and Patrick Henry, among others—were heard throughout the colonies. They questioned the right of England to rule America so harshly. They insisted that their own rights be respected. A group in Massachusetts formed the Sons of

Liberty to oppose these taxes by any means they could. Women and girls organized the Daughters of Liberty. They spun their own thread on spinning wheels to avoid buying British-made cloth, clearly breaking the law.

As hated as the taxes were, even worse was the threat of the Quartering Act. Parliament had decreed that British soldiers could be housed with colonists against their will, intimidating them and invading their privacy.

Gradually, many colonists came to see that they were together in their opposition to hateful English laws and an unsympathetic Parliament. They realized they had more in common with each other than geography. They formed

MORE ABOUT THE STAMP ACT

The Stamp Act of 1765 was one way England planned on paying its debts from the French and Indian War. The act stated that all important documents, journals, pamphlets, and playing cards be marked with stamps purchased from the British government. Irked by Britain's thoughtless demands, the colonists revolted by mobbing ships carrying stamped papers. They disregarded the law and banned English goods as well. This resistance, as well as the interference on the part of sympathetic lawmakers and merchants, resulted in the repeal of the Stamp Act in March 1766. However, England also established supreme power over the colonies, which angered the colonists and led to the American Revolution.

Committees of Correspondence to send letters to like-minded people to let each other know what was going on in their colony and how angry they felt about it. Express riders (Paul Revere was the best known) took these messages from one town to another.

For some, letter writing was not enough. Colonial leaders wanted to meet with each other in person to confer about their problems with Great Britain. The Stamp Act of 1765 gave them their first opportunity. The Stamp Act required that all paper—legal documents, licenses, contracts, newspapers, pamphlets, and even playing cards—carry a stamp paid for by a tax. Outraged colonists called for a "congress" to discuss the issue. At that time, a "congress" simply meant a "conference." It was not a governing body but a group of men coming together to share their ideas. They hoped that their meeting would get the sympathetic attention of the Crown.

It had the opposite effect. Parliament refused to recognize that a colonial congress had any authority and continued to pass new taxes. In response to a new tax on tea in December 1773, Boston patriots stole aboard British ships in the harbor and dumped cases

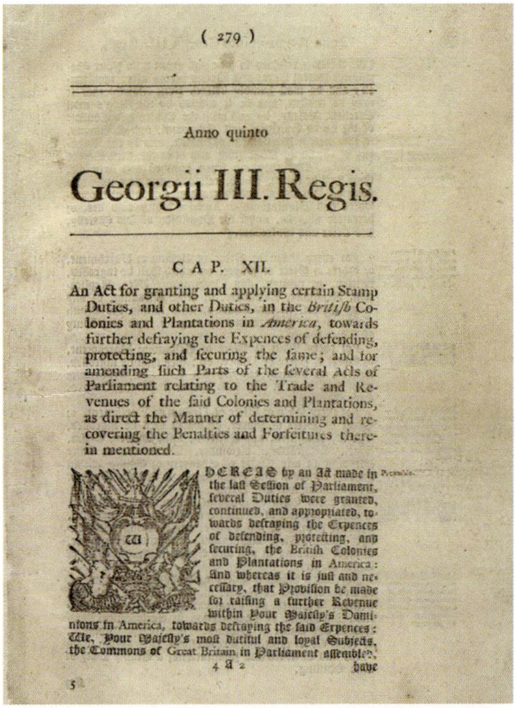

(279)

Anno quinto

Georgii III. Regis.

CAP. XII.

An Act for granting and applying certain Stamp Duties, and other Duties, in the *Britiſh* Colonies and Plantations in *America*, towards further defraying the Expences of defending, protecting, and ſecuring the ſame; and for amending ſuch Parts of the ſeveral Acts of Parliament relating to the Trade and Revenues of the ſaid Colonies and Plantations, as direct the Manner of determining and recovering the Penalties and Forfeitures therein mentioned.

WHEREAS by an Act made in the laſt Seſſion of Parliament, ſeveral Duties were granted, continued, and appropriated, towards defraying the Expences of defending, protecting, and ſecuring, the Britiſh Colonies and Plantations in America: And whereas it is juſt and neceſſary, that Proviſion be made for raiſing a further Revenue within Your Majeſty's Dominions in America, towards defraying the ſaid Expences: We, Your Majeſty's moſt dutiful and loyal Subjects, the Commons of Great Britain in Parliament aſſembled, have

4 A 2

The Stamp Act stated that all documents, journals, pamphlets, and even playing cards must have a taxed stamp.

of tea into the water. As punishment for the "tea party," Parliament closed the port of Boston to all shipping. The Massachusetts legislature, supported by those in Rhode Island and Virginia, declared this act "intolerable." Patriots prepared to fight back with muskets.

But before they rushed to war, colonial leaders called for another meeting, a Continental Congress. Some colonies elected delegates to the congress openly; others appointed them secretly. Some delegates were loyal to the king; some were not. All of them cared very much about the future of America.

CHAPTER TWO

A CONTINENTAL CONGRESS IS CONVENED

Delegates from each of the colonies except for Georgia gathered in Philadelphia in September 1774. Excitement and worry about the future filled the air. The delegates were greeted with warmth and so many dinner parties that John Adams referred to Philadelphia as a "city of feasts."

"This is a young, smart, spirited body," Adams wrote in his diary about the men he met. Silas Deane of Connecticut confided to his wife on September 1, "We are in high spirits." Joseph Galloway of Pennsylvania was a little

John Adams served as the nation's first vice president from 1789 until 1797 and its second president from 1797 until 1801.

more cautious. He wrote to the governor of New Jersey in early September, "I think [the Congress] will behave with Temper and Moderation."

It was expected that the meeting would be short. Colonial legislatures had instructed the delegates what to do. For instance, New Hampshire delegates were told to

> devise, consult, and adopt measures, as may have the most likely tendency to extricate the Colonies from their present difficulties; to secure and perpetuate their rights, liberties, and privileges, and to restore that peace, harmony, and mutual confidence which once happily subsisted between the parent country and her Colonies.

The majority of delegates wanted to restore peace between the colonies and England, not to declare their independence from the Crown. However, they also wanted to preserve their rights, even if that meant war. Most were confident that once King George III heard how unhappy the colonists were, he would repeal the hateful laws. A few radicals from Massachusetts and Virginia muttered about political freedom but did so very quietly.

THE DELEGATES WHO SERVED

Although the delegates knew of each other by reputation and through the Committees of Correspondence, most had never met, because travel between the colonies was so difficult. They carried with them the opinions of their friends and neighbors and intended to protect the interests of their own neighborhoods and their own colonies.

KING GEORGE III

George William Frederick was born on June 4, 1738, in London and died on January 20, 1820, at Windsor Castle near London. His actions incited the American Revolution when he refused to give in to any of the colonies' demands. After emerging victorious from the French and Indian War, which was the American portion of the larger, international Seven Years' War, George insisted on taxing the colonies to recoup war debts. Even as the colonists were winning the revolution, George stubbornly continued until America had won its independence. He suffered from a disease called porphyria, which interrupted his rule with compromised health. By the time he died, he was blind, deaf, and mad.

Joshua Reynolds painted this portrait of George III in 1779. It shows him wearing full ceremonial robes and holding a scepter.

Many of the men who served during the First or Second Continental Congress have since become familiar to Americans as the Founding Fathers: John Adams, Benjamin Franklin, Thomas Jefferson, John Hancock, and Richard Henry Lee, for instance. But most of the three hundred delegates that served over the Continental Congress's fourteen-year history are not well known today.

Among the first delegates were twenty-five lawyers, twelve merchants, four physicians, two farmers, nine landowners, and one minister. One half of the men were college graduates, which was remarkable for that time.

Payton Randolph, the speaker of Virginia's House of Burgesses (America's first representative legislature), was unanimously elected presiding officer at the first Congress. There would be thirteen presidents after him. Charles Thomson of Philadelphia was named secretary. Thomson served as secretary until the Congress was dissolved in 1789, faithfully taking notes at each session, copying petitions, and writing letters, all in longhand with a quill pen. Everything was carefully saved, and when the papers of the Continental Congress were collected, they made up 170,000 manuscript pages.

Delegates adopted a rule of secrecy that was closely followed. This allowed them to speak their minds freely, without fear of arrest. Until independence was accepted by England, they were considered traitors and could have been arrested and taken to England for trial.

FOUNDATION

The Congress had to invent itself. It was a new organization, and the delegates had to decide its purpose. Was it to advise the colonies only? Could it take action? Could it make binding laws? Must all delegates agree on a proposal, or would the majority rule? Were they to follow parliamentary procedure or make their own?

If they voted by colony, instead of as individual delegates, would each colony have the same number of votes, or should votes be allocated on the basis of population, trade revenue, or geographic size of the colony?

Patrick Henry reminded the gathering that this was the first general congress in the 150 years of colonial history, and they had to make their own rules. They should not act as the English Parliament did, because conditions in America were much different than those in England.

Henry urged the delegates to think nationally. John Adams recorded in his diary on September 5 that Henry had declared, "The distinctions between Virginia, New York, and New England are no more. I am not a Virginian, but an American." Henry's words were very influential and started delegates thinking of themselves as "American," too, rather than as New Yorkers or Pennsylvanians.

Colonists were most concerned with their rights and how they were being violated. They felt they had the same rights as all Englishmen, based on the British constitution and the colonial charters. "Emigrants do not leave their allegiances when they leave their native land," Richard Henry Lee of Virginia argued, according to John Adams. He believed they should still be citizens of their native land no matter where they lived.

After a few weeks of discussion, one committee was formed to list the colonists' rights and another to list their grievances (complaints) to send to the king. They then combined the lists into a Declaration of Rights and Grievances. The declaration began with the recap of the events of the past ten years, since the end of the French and Indian War, emphasizing the unpopular laws passed, "all of which are impolitic [unwise], unjust, and cruel, as well as unconstitutional, and most dangerous and destructive of American rights." They pointed out that when earlier complaints were made, they were "repeatedly treated with contempt by His Majesty's ministers of state."

The petition continued:

> [O]ur ancestors, who first settled these colonies, were at the time of their emigration from the mother country, entitled to all the rights, liberties, and immunities of free and natural born subjects within the realm of England . . .
>
> That the foundation of English liberty, and of all free government, is a right in the people to participate in their legislative council . . . they are entitled to a free and exclusive power of legislation . . .
>
> In the course of our inquiry, we find many infringements and violations of the foregoing rights, which, from an ardent desire that harmony and mutual intercourse of affection and interest may be restored . . . to state such acts and measures as have been

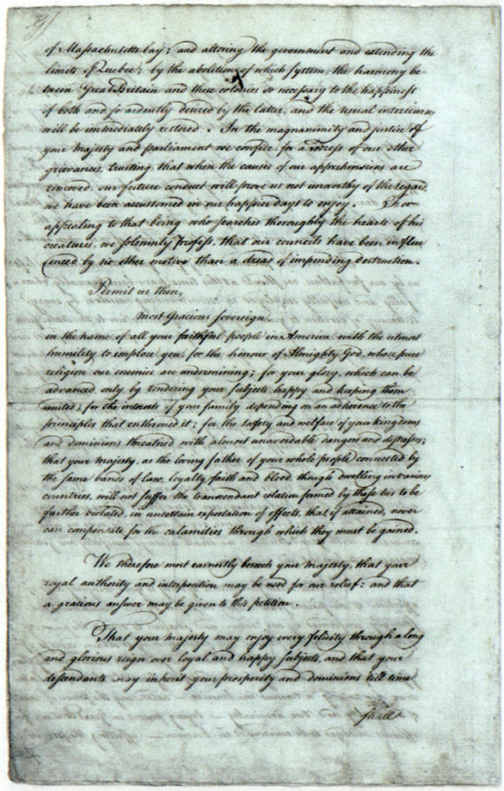

John Dickinson handwrote the petition to King George on October 26, 1774, during the First Continental Congress.

> adopted since the last war which demonstrate a system formed to enslave America.

They then listed their major grievances: taxation without representation, closing the port of Boston, and keeping a standing army in several colonies. They explained that they planned to form an association to boycott British goods and to stop exporting American ones to Britain. They would also sign a "nonconsumption" agreement, refusing to use any British goods already in the colonies.

The Declaration of Rights and Grievances was sent to King George III on October 24, 1774. The delegates went home with the hope that the king would instruct Parliament to make changes in the laws affecting the colonies. Peace would be restored, and life would go on as usual. The delegates planned to meet again in Philadelphia in the spring, on May 10, 1775, to hear the king's response.

★ CHAPTER THREE

THE CONGRESS MEETS AGAIN

Colonial agents for King George III responded to the Declaration of Rights and Grievances instead of the king himself. By dismissing the colonists' concerns, the king dissolved the delegates' remaining loyalty to him. To add insult to injury, a law from the English Parliament sought to end trade between New England and the other colonies. New Englanders refused to obey this law.

In 1774, Massachusetts patriots had formed groups of militia called minutemen. These "instant soldiers" promised to fight the red-coated British soldiers with a moment's notice. Now they were primed and ready.

On April 19, 1775, just before the second Congress gathered, British troops marched toward Concord, Massachusetts, to get the ammunition they had stored there. Express riders Paul Revere and William Dawes alerted the countryside, and the minutemen assembled. As the Americans marched toward Lexington, they encountered British troops. The first shot was fired—no one is sure by whom—and the American Revolution (1775–1783) began.

The First Shots by William Barnes Wollen shows minutemen fighting British soldiers at Lexington Common, Massachusetts, on April 19, 1775. This was the first battle of the American Revolution.

All across the colonies, residents got ready for conflict, building arsenals of weapons. In early May, a ragtag group of soldiers called the Green Mountain Boys marched to the British-held Fort Ticonderoga in northern New York. They took the undermanned fort easily and captured cannons that they dragged back to Massachusetts for the defense of Boston. More cannons and ammunition were captured at the British garrison at Crown Point a little farther north, on Lake Champlain. Militia groups formed in other colonies and looked for opportunities to capture weapons.

A CAREFULLY CONSIDERED RESPONSE

As the delegates listened to the responses of the king's agents in May 1775, they were aware of the rebellion that seethed around them. They also understood that no changes would be made in their favor. The king would continue to ignore their grievances, and Parliament would continue to make laws without asking for their input.

Deciding what to do about the situation seemed to take an unnecessarily long time because the Congress had agreed that each delegate not only had a right to speak on each issue but had a duty to do so as well. Each man had opinions on the regulations governing trade, personal liberty, loyalty, and the power of the Congress to make laws and wage a war. All delegates received a steady stream of letters and newspapers from home. The delegates felt they were representing these constituents, so they read their letters carefully and repeated their ideas during the long discussions. This procedure became the basis of representative democracy: the insistence that all opinions matter and that elected officials must consider the opinions of voters.

For an impatient and impulsive man like John Adams, the wait was frustrating. He wrote to a friend on May 21, 1775, "Our unwieldy body moves very slow. We shall do something in Time, but must have our own Way."

Although most of the delegates realized a break with England was impossible to avoid, some insisted that they try to reach the king one more time before they initiated a full-scale war. In July 1775, John Dickinson of Pennsylvania wrote the Olive Branch Petition, asking the king to repeal the hated laws. The petition stated that it would be necessary to resort to arms to get the king's attention but promised that the fighting would end as soon as the British government met their demands.

King George ignored the petition. In August 1775, he issued a proclamation declaring the colonies to be in a state of rebellion. He ordered his officers and loyal subjects to suppress the revolt "and bring the traitors to justice," as he wrote. From his point of view, American "patriots" were traitors and should be jailed or executed.

It was clear to the delegates by then that they must formally unite in their opposition to the king. They talked for hours about how they could forge thirteen individual colonies into one nation. Other than hatred for oppression, what did they have in common? It was necessary that they find common ground before going forward.

They knew they had to defend themselves first. Many British soldiers were already in America, and others were on their way over. Without a colonial army and navy, the British would take over by force. Members of the Continental Congress would be arrested and sent to England for trial.

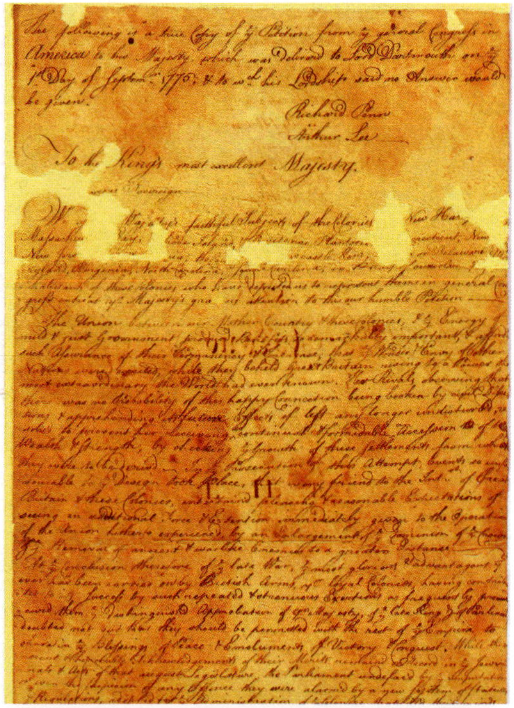
The following is a true Copy of the Petition from the general Congress in America to his Majesty which was delivered to Lord Dartmouth on the 1st Day of Septem. 1775; & to which his Lordship said no Answer would be given.

Richard Penn
Arthur Lee

To the King's most excellent Majesty.

The Olive Branch Petition was signed by forty-eight congressional delegates. See transcription on page 51.

THE OLIVE BRANCH

The petition known as the Olive Branch was drafted by John Dickinson and signed on July 8, 1775, by forty-eight members of the Continental Congress. Representatives from all of the original colonies but Rhode Island gave King George one last chance to avoid a war for independence by asserting the rights of colonists while remaining loyal to the crown. Unfortunately for the fate of England, the king ignored the petition, declaring in a speech to Parliament on October 26, 1775: "It is now become the part of wisdom … to put a speedy end to these disorders by the most decisive exertions."

In mid-June 1775, John Adams proposed that a Continental army be raised. The Congress unanimously selected George Washington to be the commander in chief. The Virginian had impressed all the delegates with his quiet determination and courage. In the early days of the conflict, Adams reported that Washington had said, "I will raise one thousand men, subsist them at my own expense, and march myself at their head for the relief of Boston."

Six months after an army of fifteen thousand men was established, a navy was authorized. Because there wasn't time to build warships, Congress authorized privateering—taking over private ships and converting them into warships. The new navy was instructed to capture English ships in the West Indies and bring the cargo back to the

This painting by Edward P. Moran shows General George Washington and the Continental army troops at Valley Forge, Pennsylvania, during the brutal winter of 1777 to 1778.

United States. If the cargo was rum, it could be sold and the money given to Congress; a cargo of guns could be used by the army.

To raise money for the war, Congress approved issuing paper money without gold to back it up, something it would later regret.

With the framework for fighting a war in place, the delegates turned their minds to the most pressing issue of all: Should they make an official break from England?

CHAPTER FOUR

THE DECLARATION OF INDEPENDENCE

Patrick Henry gives his famous, passionate speech to the Virginia Convention on March 23, 1775.

The winter of 1775 and the following spring saw fierce, frequent discussions as the debate over whether to declare independence from Great Britain continued. Some colonists wanted England to remain in control, while others wanted free of such control at once.

On March 20, Joseph Hewes of North Carolina wrote, "We do not treat each other with that decency and respect that was observed heretofore. Jealousies, ill-natured observations and recriminations take the place of reason and argument. Our Tempers are soured."

GIVE ME LIBERTY

Patrick Henry (1736-1799) was a lawyer, orator, and statesman who dedicated most of his life to Virginia politics. In addition to serving as a delegate for the First and Second Continental Congresses, he took on the role of the first governor of the Commonwealth of Virginia from 1776 to 1779. Writing about the First Continental Congress, John Adams said, "there was not one member, except Patrick Henry, who appeared ... sensible of the Precipice [cliff] or rather the Pinnacle [high rock] on which We stood, and had candor and courage enough to acknowledge it."

On March 23, 1775, Patrick Henry addressed the second Virginia Convention. Radically opposed to the British government, Henry used his exceptional gifts as a public speaker to convince the delegates of the Continental Congress that independence from England was the best solution. The words he spoke have become some of the most famous in American history: "I know not what course others may taken, but as for me, give me liberty or give me death."

Despite his opposition to the practice of slavery, Henry owned several slaves, one of which cared for Henry's ailing wife, Sarah, who died in 1775. Henry remarried in 1777 and fathered a total of seventeen children. He turned down positions on the Supreme Court and as secretary of state and retired from public life in 1791.

A month later, Samuel Adams of Massachusetts wrote that he was still hearing of the need for reconciliation with England, noting, "I am exceedingly disgusted when I hear it mentioned . . . The only Alternative is Independency or Slavery."

James Duane of New York and James Wilson of Pennsylvania spoke against a break with England at this time. They believed there was no rush, even if it was inevitable. The colonies weren't ready for independence. "Before we are prepared to build the new house, why should we pull down the old one, and expose ourselves to all the inclemencies [severity] of the season?" they wrote.

There were many other questions to be answered, from how to create a post office to deliver mail to how to raise money for running this new government without taxes. What kind of national offices would be needed? Without a structure of royalty, as there was in England, how would a hierarchy of importance be achieved? How would a judiciary system be developed? And how would they establish relations with other nations?

Others felt it was more important to achieve independence first; the details could come later. Months went by with much talk and no action.

THE DEBATE CONTINUES

The colonial legislatures moved faster on the issue than the national body did. In April 1776, the North Carolina legislature authorized its delegation to vote for independence. The next month, the Virginia House of Burgesses forced the question by passing a resolution that the Continental Congress vote on independence immediately. The resolution sat for several days on the desk of Virginia's delegate, Richard Henry Lee, while he decided how and when to introduce it.

Massachusetts delegate Samuel Adams wrote to a friend on June 6, "Tomorrow a motion will be made, and a Question I hope decided, the most important that was ever agitated in America." The next day, Lee introduced a resolution urging the Congress to declare its independence from Great Britain. It was worded simply:

> That these United Colonies are, and of right ought to be, free and independent States, that they are absolved from all allegiance to the British Crown, and that all political connection between them and the State of Great Britain is, and ought to be, totally dissolved.
>
> That it is expedient forthwith to take the most effectual measures for forming foreign Alliances.
>
> That a plan of confederation be prepared and transmitted to the respective Colonies for their consideration and approbation.

There was no certainty the resolution would pass. On June 8, South Carolina delegate Edward Rutledge wrote to John Jay of New York. "The Congress sat till 8 o'clock this evening in consequence of a motion of R. H. Lee rendering ourselves free and independent State. The sensible part of the House opposed the Motion… they saw no Wisdom in a Declaration of Independence," which would alert Great Britain to such a plan.

Jefferson wrote later in his "Account of a Declaration" that he was nervous about the vote. "The people of the middle colonies (Maryland, Delaware, Pennsylvania, New Jersey, and New York) were not ripe for bidding adieu to British connection." The middle colonies, as well as South Carolina, benefited the most from the mercantile system and considered themselves far removed from the problems in New England.

"Congress never were so much engaged as at this time," wrote William Whipple of New Hampshire on June 10. "[B]usiness presses on them exceedingly . . . There are so many irons in the fire, I fear some of them will burn."

The best argument for declaring independence was the need to create alliances with other nations, particularly France, for help against the British army. If they remained British colonies, they could not expect to find support anywhere in Europe.

Congressional leaders felt that all the colonies had to agree to independence. Just one colony against independence might give aid to the enemy, and the war would be lost. Most of those who voted "nay" in the early votes did not oppose the idea of separation from Great Britain, but they didn't want a declaration made until all the colonies supported it fully.

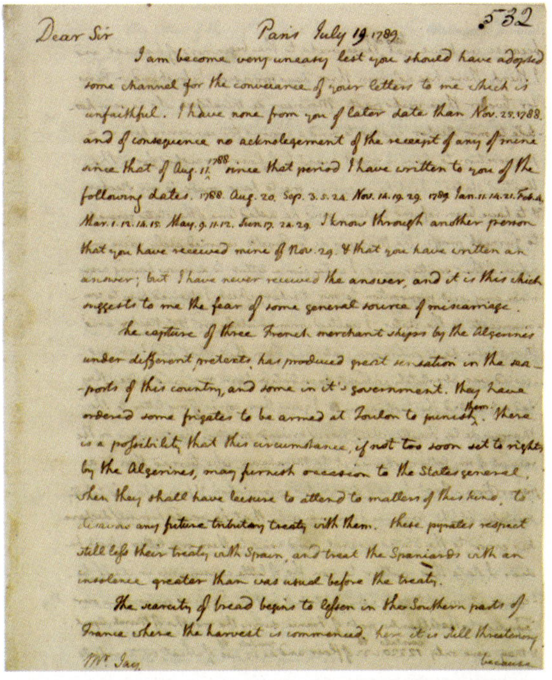

532

Dear Sir Paris July 19. 1789.

I am become very uneasy lest you should have adopted some channel for the conveyance of your letters to me which is unfaithful. I have none from you of later date than Nov. 25. 1788. and of consequence no acknolegement of the receipt of any of mine since that of Aug. 11. 1788. since that period I have written to you of the following dates. 1788. Aug. 20. Sep. 3. 5. 24. Nov. 14. 19. 29. 1789. Jan. 11. 14. 21. Feb. 4. Mar. 1. 12. 14. 15. May. 9. 11. 12. June 17. 24. 29. I know through another person that you have received mine of Nov. 29. & that you have written an answer; but I have never received the answer, and it is this which suggests to me the fear of some general source of miscarriage.

The capture of three French merchant ships by the Algerines under different pretexts, has produced great sensation in the sea-ports of this country, and some in it's government. they have ordered some frigates to be armed at Toulon to punish them. there is a possibility that this circumstance, if not too soon set to rights by the Algerines, may furnish occasion to the States general, when they shall have leisure to attend to matters of this kind, to discuss any future tributary treaty with them. these pyrates respect still less their treaty with Spain, and treat the Spaniards with an insolence greater than was usual before the treaty.

The scarcity of bread begins to lessen in the Southern parts of France where the harvest is commenced. here it is still threatening

Mr. Jay

Thomas Jefferson reported on the French Revolution to Secretary of Foreign Affairs John Jay in this letter.

PREPARING THE DECLARATION

On June 11, 1776, Congress appointed a committee to begin preparing a formal declaration in case the votes changed. Thomas Jefferson, John Adams, Benjamin Franklin, Roger

Sherman, and Robert Livingston were appointed to draft the document.

Meanwhile, another committee was appointed to draw up the Articles of Confederation, the second part of Lee's resolution, to organize the operation of the new government. Thus, when one government was dissolved, another would be ready to take its place. On June 17, the name of the confederation was proposed and accepted. The new nation would be known as the United States of America.

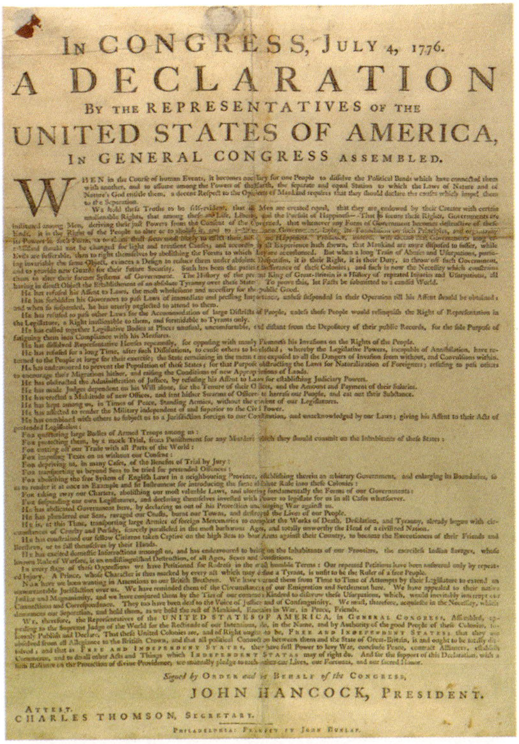
IN CONGRESS, JULY 4, 1776.
A DECLARATION
BY THE REPRESENTATIVES OF THE
UNITED STATES OF AMERICA,
IN GENERAL CONGRESS ASSEMBLED.

Signed by ORDER and in BEHALF of the CONGRESS,
JOHN HANCOCK, PRESIDENT.
ATTEST.
CHARLES THOMSON, SECRETARY.
PHILADELPHIA: PRINTED BY JOHN DUNLAP.

The first printed text of the Declaration of Independence is the Dunlap Broadside. See transcript on page 52.

As the time to vote on the independence resolution neared, John Adams wrote, "We are now in the very midst of a revolution, the most completely unexpected, and remarkable of any in the history of nations." Most likely, the other delegates agreed with him.

"I expect the grand question will be determined in Congress [on June 28]," William Whipple wrote, "that being the day assigned to receive the report of a Committee who are preparing the Declaration."

On that day, the draft of the Declaration of Independence was read to the Congress. It began with a preamble:

> When in the Course of human events it becomes necessary for one people to dissolve the political bonds which have connected them with another, and assume among the powers of the earth, the separate and equal station to which the Laws of Nature and Nature's God entitle them, a decent respect to the opinions of mankind requires that they should declare the causes which impel them to the separation.
>
> We hold these truths to be self-evident, that all men are created equal, that they are endowed by their Creator with certain inalienable Rights, that among these are Life, Liberty and the pursuit of Happiness.—That to secure these rights, Governments are instituted among Men, deriving their just powers from the consent of the governed.—That whenever any Form of Government becomes destructive of these ends, it is the Right of the People to alter or to abolish it, and to institute new Government, laying its foundation on such principles.

Then followed a restatement of the grievances the colonies had suffered, but there was now no hint of reconciliation. They were simply listed as reasons for dissolving the bonds between the two nations. As the delegates listened to the declaration, they made notes about what to add, cut, or rewrite. Then the document went back to the committee for revision.

THE OFFICIAL VOTE

Two votes were necessary to make independence from England official. One vote was on Lee's resolution to end allegiance to the British Crown; the other was to accept the written Declaration of Independence. Congress had decided that each colony (rather than each delegate) would have one vote. Within each colonial delegation of three to five members, individuals might vote against the measure, but the majority had to accept it for their "yea" vote to count. Unless all the colonies voted for it, the issue would be dropped.

The vote on the independence resolution came on July 2, 1776. Nine colonies had promised to vote for it: New Hampshire, Connecticut, Massachusetts, Rhode Island, New Jersey, Maryland, Virginia, North Carolina, and Georgia. New York and Pennsylvania were waiting for instructions from their state legislators and would not vote. South Carolina was against the resolution but agreed to vote for it if all the other colonies did.

Delaware had a three-man delegation. One man was for, the other was against, and the third was absent. To break the tie and ensure that Delaware's vote would be for independence, absent delegate Caesar Rodney rode all night, arriving in Philadelphia just in time to cast his vote. The colonies were united on the vote for the resolution, with no "nays" being recorded. Delegate Robert Treat Paine of Massachusetts noted in his diary on July 2, "The Independence of the State Voted and declared."

On July 4, the Congress voted to accept the wording of Jefferson's declaration without discussion or celebration from the weary delegates. John Adams wrote to his wife, Abigail, "If it had been made seven months ago, it would have been attended with many great and glorious efforts."

By July 5, copies of the Declaration of Independence were being distributed in New Jersey and Delaware. On July 6, the Pennsylvania Evening Post printed it in full. On July 9, General Washington ordered the Declaration of Independence read to the American army. As word

John Nixon reads the Declaration of Independence in Philadelphia on July 8, 1776, in this hand-colored woodcut.

of the declaration spread, colonists cheered, lit bonfires (sometimes burning British goods), and rang church bells.

Delegates gathered in Philadelphia on August 2, 1776, to sign the document. The Declaration of Independence closed with the ringing words, "We mutually pledge to each other our lives, our fortunes, and our sacred honor." The signers knew that if their struggle for independence failed, their property would be confiscated and they could be executed. Indeed, over the course of the war, five were arrested (including three of the four signers from South Carolina), ten lost their homes, and seventeen lost other property. The war years ahead would be very difficult for all the colonists, but no one suggested giving in.

★ CHAPTER FIVE

WAR BREAKS OUT

The reality of waging war became clear once the excitement of the Declaration of Independence faded. An army had to be raised, officers appointed, supplies gathered, and funds found. And that did not even include the actual fighting.

In 1775, when the war began in Massachusetts, the Continental army wasn't an army. It was a group of boys and men who came together to keep British soldiers from taking over their farms and houses. They were not prepared to leave their work and families to fight a long war. They had had no military training and were given no uniforms, and the only weapons they carried were the ones they brought from home. No camps or forts had been established for them, and they slept on the ground or in barns when they were on the march. They found food when and where they could.

Few of the officers had been tested in battle. George Washington was an exception. He had served in the British army during the French and Indian War and knew how to lead men. Congress

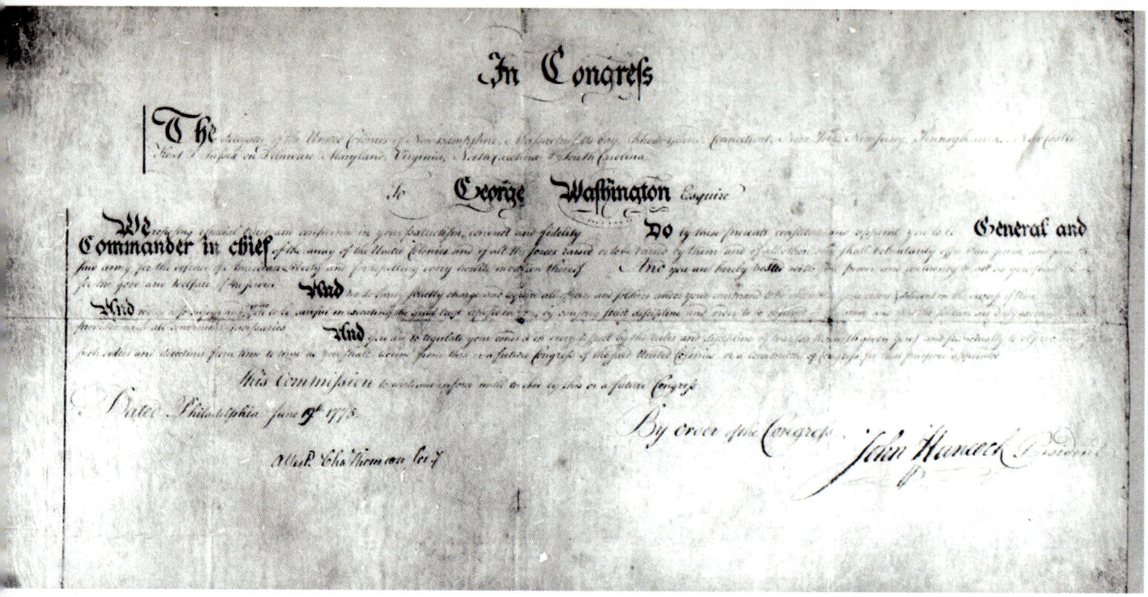
In Congress

To George Washington Esquire

General and Commander in chief

By order of the Congress

John Hancock

John Hancock and Charles Thomson signed this document appointing George Washington to the position of commander in chief of the Continental army. See transcription on page 53.

chose most of the officers from volunteers and from the recommendations of others. Disappointment and disaster were the frequent result. Many officers didn't know how to plan battles, organize camps, or command soldiers.

Oliver Wolcott of Connecticut lamented on March 22, 1777, that if the colonies had had a "Regular army . . . we probably should have been able to have crushed the British Power in America." But the army was far from "regular." Poorly trained town militia, colonial troops, and frontier sharpshooters were in the field with the Continental army.

Congress passed a law requiring each colony to recruit a certain number of men for the colonial army, but it was hard to enforce. John Adams wrote that these quotas were impossible to fill because "some colonies have such bodies of Quakers, and Mennonites, and Moravians, who

This nineteenth-century engraving by A. Bobbett shows a militiaman preparing to leave for the battles of Lexington and Concord during the American Revolution.

are principled against War, and other have such Bodies of Tories [loyal to Britain], or Cowards, or unprincipled People who will not wage War." He didn't mention that men were reluctant to sign up because they would have to leave their work and families and might not get paid to risk their lives.

READYING FOR WAR

The day after independence was declared, Joseph Hews of North Carolina wrote, "We resolve to raise regiments, resolve to make Cannon, resolve to make and import muskets, powder, and clothing, but it is a melancholy fact that near half of our men, Cannon, muskets, powder, clothes, etc., is to be found nowhere but on paper."

Finding supplies was just as hard as finding men. Congress asked the colonies for supplies first, and when that didn't work, it tried to buy or borrow them, and as a last resort, it took them. Farmers were required to give a percentage of their crops to feed soldiers. Horses were frequently requisitioned for the troops.

The British knew how important supplies were and went after colonial storerooms. In May 1777, they destroyed seventeen hundred barrels of salted meat and one thousand barrels of flour, a devastating loss to the new army. "Powder! Powder!" was the never-ending call from the front lines, where unarmed soldiers were useless.

The congressmen hoped that Canada would join the colonies in the rebellion, adding needed manpower and supplies. They were disappointed to find that most Canadians wanted to remain loyal to England. Even worse, Americans loyal to the Crown (Tories) flocked to Canada, seeking safety from angry rebels. According to Edmund C. Burnett's book, *The Continental Congress*, John Adams said of English sympathizers: "A Tory here is the most despicable animal in the creation. Spiders, toads, snakes are their only proper emblems."

During the six years of war, the Continental Congress had to move its meeting place frequently to keep out of the line of fire from the advancing British army. It went from Philadelphia to Baltimore, Maryland; to York and Lancaster, Pennsylvania; to Princeton, New Jersey; and to Annapolis, Maryland, before returning to Philadelphia.

Daily dispatches kept Congress, wherever it was, informed of the military campaigns. Rumors ran through Congress, and sometimes members had to wait days

MONEY MATTERS

The Continental Congress printed its own money to cover the cost of the war. Continentals, as they were called, became worthless almost immediately because there was no gold or silver to back them up. They were investments in the future of America, backed by the hope of future tax monies, and would be redeemable only when the colonies broke from England. Issuing Continentals was another way America declared its independence. It was the first time money used by the colonies wasn't marked with the faces of European royalty. In 1785, the Continental Congress adopted the dollar as the unit for national currency. "Not worth a Continental" became a popular expression to describe something that lacked value.

to learn the truth. News from the front kept members alternating between despair and elation. They were constantly distressed over the high number of deserters and the terrible conditions at camps like Valley Forge.

The medical department of Congress had to find ways to keep the soldiers as healthy as possible. Smallpox, dysentery, influenza, and other infections killed thousands of men. Little effective medicine was available. The lack of decent food or housing, exhaustion, and cold killed many, as well. Unheated barns were converted into hospitals, and no nursing care was available.

FINDING FUNDS

Finding the money to pay for a government was always a challenge for Congress. At that time, silver or gold coins (specie) were used for most financial transactions. Bills of credit were issued for large purchases and then paid off in specie. Congress estimated the cost of the war at \$5 million, an impossibly large sum then. America did not have enough specie to pay for a war, so Congress issued bills of credit and authorized the printing of paper money without gold or silver to back it up.

The paper money, called Continentals, became almost worthless. In January 1777, when it was first issued, \$1.25 in paper money was worth \$1.00 in silver or gold.

These images of the front and back of a five-dollar bill are examples of the currency printed by the Continental Congress to cover the war's cost. They became worthless almost immediately.

Five years later, it took $167.50 in paper money to buy a dollar's worth of specie. Gradually, the worthless money was taken out of circulation.

Congress did not have the power to tax then, so it asked for contributions from the states. Most states planned to use what money they had for their own needs and were unable or unwilling to pay the nation's debts. In 1781, the nation was almost bankrupt, and Congress suspended all payments. Soldiers who hadn't been paid for months were near mutiny. It was only their high regard for General Washington that kept them in the field.

INTERNATIONAL MATTERS

Congress wanted the new nation to be recognized by Europe. In the early years, the Committee of Secret Correspondence was responsible for dealing with European leaders, trying to make alliances and find financial support. Later, the committee was called the Committee on Foreign Affairs, and eventually it became the State Department.

During the war, members of Congress were sent to Spain, France, the Netherlands, Austria, and Russia on diplomatic missions. They found the most sympathetic ear in France, England's longtime enemy. In July 1780, six thousand French soldiers arrived in Rhode Island, led by the Marquis de Lafayette. This support, as well as the money France loaned to the United States, was crucial to the nation's victory.

THE END OF THE WAR

On October 21, 1781, an express rider brought the news to Congress that the British commander, Lord Cornwallis, had surrendered his entire army to General Washington in Yorktown, Virginia. British and American representatives negotiated a peace treaty, the Treaty of Paris, in the fall of 1782 that was finalized on September 3, 1783.

The agreement stated that Great Britain would keep Canada, that those in America who had stayed loyal to England would be protected from revenge, and that English merchants would be paid for old debts. In return, England acknowledged the independence of the United States and agreed to give up its claims to western lands as far as the Mississippi River.

The war had hurt the American economy badly. For six years, all trade had been halted. From Boston fisheries to South Carolina rice fields, the nation had suffered. Now it was time to rebuild.

★ CHAPTER SIX

THE TASK OF GOVERNMENT

Once the war was won, the Continental Congress had the important but difficult job of establishing a new system of government. This work continued through much of the 1780s, with many delays and debates.

REMOVING THE ARTICLES OF CONFEDERATION

The Articles of Confederation had been adopted by Congress in 1777 and ratified by the states in 1781. The delegates knew there would be problems with the articles before they

To all to whom

The Articles of Confederation were adopted by Congress on November 15, 1777. See transcription on page 54.

adopted them, but they were under great pressure to set up some form of government in a hurry. Because of their experience with King George III, most delegates were afraid that a strong central government would turn into a tyranny as bad as the English monarchy. They wanted to be certain their new government would have limited powers. But they limited its powers so much that it became almost powerless.

The articles created a national government with a single house of Congress where each state, regardless of population, had one vote. Small states didn't want to take a chance on being outvoted, so they insisted this provision be included. Large states thought this was unfair. While there were only thirteen votes in Congress, there were many more delegates, and delegates from the same state rarely agreed on issues, causing many problems in the voting.

There was no chief executive officer (national president), and this meant that Congress had to perform every executive function, an impossible task. It couldn't pass laws and oversee how they were followed.

Congress had few powers that affected the entire nation. It could declare war and negotiate peace; it could raise armed forces; and it could control the development of the western territories. Each state had more power than the national government in regulating commerce and levying taxes. The states could ignore federal laws because they were not enforced.

Nine of the thirteen states had to agree to any federal law Congress might enact before it could become a law, including issuing stamps and minting coins. While Congress could request money from the states, the states had the right to refuse to give it to Congress. Without money, the government could not issue back pay to the soldiers who fought in the war or pay the merchants who had given supplies, food, and ammunition to the army on credit. And until the debts were paid, Congress could make no plans for the future.

Congress was given the authority to mediate disputes between the states, which should have been the job of a judicial system. Listening to petty cases took up much of its time.

Congress could not regulate trade. Each state had its own system of trade regulations, which made trading with the United States very difficult for foreign countries. The port of Charleston had one set of regulations, the port of New York another, and the port of Boston still another.

After five years of trying to govern the nation under the Articles of Confederation, Congress was discouraged. James Manning and Nathan Miller reported to their home state of Rhode Island on September 28, 1786, "It is now agreed by all that our federal Government is but a name; a meer shadow without any substance; and we think it our duty to inform the State that it is totally inefficient for the purposes of the Union."

The US Constitution replaced the Articles of Confederation. It was written in 1787 and ratified in 1788.

THE BILL OF RIGHTS

During the debates that took place while the Constitution was being written, a frequent argument was that it could allow the central government to establish tyranny in much the same way that the British had violated colonists' rights before and during the American Revolution. The congressmen pushed for a bill of rights that spelled out the protections of individual citizens. Several states refused to ratify the Constitution unless a bill of rights was promptly passed.

Twelve amendments were originally proposed, but only ten made their way into the Constitution, becoming its first amendments. Known as the Bill of Rights, these articles were ratified on December 15, 1791.

A NEW PLAN

With the complaints getting louder, several congressmen met in Annapolis, Maryland, in February 1787 to discuss the situation. They decided that instead of trying to modify the articles to make them work, they would start over and write a totally new plan for the government. A Constitutional Convention was held in Philadelphia between May and September of 1787. Under the direction of James Madison, the convention wrote the present US Constitution. It was ratified the following year.

The new Congress would have two houses, a Senate and a House of Representatives. Two senators would be elected from each state, and representatives were elected based on population. A chief executive officer would be elected through an electoral college, and an independent judiciary would be set up. This is the system used today, and it works so well it has been copied by many other nations.

The Continental Congress met for the last time on October 10, 1788. Its final act was to grant 10 square acres (4.05 hectares) of land just north of Virginia for the creation of a federal town. It would become known as Washington, DC. Until the new capital city was complete, the new Congress would meet in New York City.

This 1793 engraving is a hand-colored woodcut that shows Washington, DC, as it was originally laid out.

The Continental Congress secretary, Charles Thomson, closed "the Journal of the United States in Congress Assembled" to formally end the session. He then rode on horseback to Mount Vernon, Virginia, and notified George Washington that he had been elected the first president of the United States. Washington would be inaugurated in March 1789.

Americans in 1789 were confident that their new government would bring them peace and prosperity. Through years of debate, trial and error, a war, and economic hard times, they had built a system of representative democracy that would be flexible enough to take them through all the good times and bad that lay ahead of them.

TIMELINE

1763 War between England and France (French and Indian War) ends.

1764 Colonists react to a tax on sugar with a boycott.

1765 Parliament passes the Stamp Act, angering colonists who declare "no taxation without representation." The Quartering Act allows British troops to be housed in American homes. The Sons of Liberty is organized to oppose British laws.

1767 Parliament passes the Townshend Acts, which enacts taxes on glass, lead, paint, paper, and tea; Samuel Adams writes letters of protest that circulate in the colonies.

1772 Committees of Correspondence continue the letter-writing campaign.

1773 The Boston Tea Party destroys British property.

1774 Parliament passes the Coercive Acts, or the Intolerable Acts, and orders the port of Boston closed. The First Continental Congress meets in Philadelphia and sends a Declaration of Rights and Grievances to George III. Minutemen are organized in New England.

1775 War with Britain begins. The second Continental Congress convenes in Philadelphia.

1776 The Declaration of Independence ends colonial allegiance to Great Britain.

1777 Congress adopts the Articles of Confederation.

1781 The Articles of Confederation are ratified. Cornwallis surrenders to Washington at Yorktown, Virginia.

1782 The Treaty of Paris ends the war between Great Britain and the United States.

1787 The US Constitution is written to take the place of the ineffective Articles of Confederation.

1789 George Washington takes office as the first president of the United States.

OLIVE BRANCH PETITION OF 1775
TRANSCRIPTION EXCERPT

July 8, 1775
To the King's Most Excellent Majesty.
The union between our Mother Country and these Colonies, and the energy of mild and just Government, produce benefits so remarkably important, and afforded such an assurance of their permanency and increase, that the wonder and envy of other nations were excited, while they beheld Great Britain rising to a power the most extra-ordinary the world had ever known.

Knowing to what violent resentments and incurable animosities civil discords are apt to exasperate and inflame the contending parties, we think ourselves required by indispensable obligations to Almighty God, to your Majesty, to our fellow-subjects, and to ourselves, immediately to use all the means in our power, not incompatible with our safety, for stopping the further effusion of blood, and for averting the impending calamities that threaten the British Empire.

Attached to your Majesty's person, family, and Government, with all devotion that principle and affection can inspire; connected with Great Britain by the strongest ties that can unite societies, and deploring every event that tends in any degree to weaken them, we solemnly assure your Majesty, that we not only most ardently desire the former harmony between her and these Colonies may be restored, but that a concord may be established between them upon so firm a basis as to perpetuate its blessings, uninterrupted by any future dissensions.

We therefore beseech your Majesty, that your royal authority and influence may be graciously interposed to procure us relief from our afflicting fears and jealousies, occasioned by the system before-mentioned, and to settle peace through every part of our Dominions, with all humility submitting to your Majesty's wise consideration, whether it may not be expedient, for facilitating those important purposes, that your Majesty be pleased to direct some mode, by which the united applications of your faithful Colonists to the Throne, in pursuance of their common counsels, may be improved into a happy and permanent reconciliation; and that, in the mean time, measures may be taken for preventing the further destruction of the lives of your Majesty's subjects; and that such statutes as more immediately distress any of your Majesty's Colonies may be repealed.

For such arrangements as your Majesty's wisdom can form for collecting the united sense of your American people, we are convinced your Majesty would receive such satisfactory proofs of the disposition of the Colonists towards their Sovereign and Parent State, that the wished for opportunity would soon be restored to them, of evincing the sincerity of their professions, by every testimony of devotion becoming the most dutiful subjects, and the most affectionate Colonists.

DECLARATION OF INDEPENDENCE (DUNLAP BROADSIDE) TRANSCRIPTION

Declaration of Independence
IN CONGRESS, July 4, 1776.
The unanimous Declaration of the thirteen united States of America,
When in the Course of human events, it becomes necessary for one people to dissolve the political bands which have connected them with another, and to assume among the powers of the earth, the separate and equal station to which the Laws of Nature and of Nature's God entitle them, a decent respect to the opinions of mankind requires that they should declare the causes which impel them to the separation.

We hold these truths to be self-evident, that all men are created equal, that they are endowed by their Creator with certain unalienable Rights, that among these are Life, Liberty and the pursuit of Happiness.—That to secure these rights, Governments are instituted among Men, deriving their just powers from the consent of the governed,—That whenever any Form of Government becomes destructive of these ends, it is the Right of the People to alter or to abolish it, and to institute new Government, laying its foundation on such principles and organizing its powers in such form, as to them shall seem most likely to effect their Safety and Happiness. Prudence, indeed, will dictate that Governments long established should not be changed for light and transient causes; and accordingly all experience hath shewn, that mankind are more disposed to suffer, while evils are sufferable, than to right themselves by abolishing the forms to which they are accustomed. But when a long train of abuses and usurpations, pursuing invariably the same Object evinces a design to reduce them under absolute Despotism, it is their right, it is their duty, to throw off such Government, and to provide new Guards for their future security.—Such has been the patient sufferance of these Colonies; and such is now the necessity which constrains them to alter their former Systems of Government. The history of the present King of Great Britain is a history of repeated injuries and usurpations, all having in direct object the establishment of an absolute Tyranny over these States. To prove this, let Facts be submitted to a candid world.

We, therefore, the Representatives of the united States of America, in General Congress, Assembled, appealing to the Supreme Judge of the world for the rectitude of our intentions, do, in the Name, and by Authority of the good People of these Colonies, solemnly publish and declare, That these United Colonies are, and of Right ought to be Free and Independent States; that they are Absolved from all Allegiance to the British Crown, and that all political connection between them and the State of Great Britain, is and ought to be totally dissolved; and that as Free and Independent States, they have full Power to levy War, conclude Peace, contract Alliances, establish Commerce, and to do all other Acts and Things which Independent States may of right do. And for the support of this Declaration, with a firm reliance on the protection of divine Providence, we mutually pledge to each other our Lives, our Fortunes and our sacred Honor.

COMMISSION TO GEORGE WASHINGTON AS COMMANDER IN CHIEF, JUNE 19, 1775

TRANSCRIPTION

IN CONGRESS

THE delegates of the United Colonies of New-hampshire, Massachusetts bay, Rhode-island, Connecticut, New-York, New-Jersey, Pennsylvania, New Castle Kent & Sussex on Delaware, Maryland, Virginia, North Carolina & South Carolina

TO GEORGE WASHINGTON Esquire

WE reposing especial trust and confidence in your patriotism, conduct and fidelity Do by these presents constitute and appoint you to be GENERAL AND COMMANDER IN CHIEF of the army of the United Colonies and of all the forces raised or to be raised by them and of all others who shall voluntarily offer their service and join the said army for the defence of American Liberty and for repelling every hostile invasion thereof. And you are hereby vested with full power and authority to act as you shall think for the good and Welfare of the service.

AND we do hereby strictly charge and require all officers and soldiers under your command to be obedient to your orders & diligent in the exercise of their several dut[ies.]

AND we do also enjoin and require you to be careful in executing the great trust reposed in you, by causing strict discipline and order to be observed in th[e] army and that the soldiers are duly exercised an[d] provided with all convenient necessaries.

AND you are to regulate your conduct in every respect by the rules and discipline of war (as herewith given you) and punctually to observe and foll[ow] such orders and directions from time to time as you shall receive from this or a future Congress of the said United Colonies or a committee of Congress for that purpose appointed.

This Commission to continue inforce until revoked by this or a future Congress.
By order of the Congress JOHN HANCOCK President
Dated Philadelphia June 19th 1775.
Attest CHAS THOMSON Secy.

ARTICLES OF CONFEDERATION
TRANSCRIPTION EXCERPT

Articles of Confederation (1777)
To all to whom these Presents shall come, we the undersigned Delegates of the States affixed to our Names send greeting.

Articles of Confederation and perpetual Union between the states of New Hampshire, Massachusetts–bay Rhode Island and Providence Plantations, Connecticut, New York, New Jersey, Pennsylvania, Delaware, Maryland, Virginia, North Carolina, South Carolina and Georgia.

I. The Stile of this Confederacy shall be "The United States of America."
II. Each state retains its sovereignty, freedom, and independence, and every power, jurisdiction, and right, which is not by this Confederation expressly delegated to the United States, in Congress assembled . . .
V. For the most convenient management of the general interests of the United States, delegates shall be annually appointed in such manner as the legislatures of each State shall direct, to meet in Congress on the first Monday in November, in every year, with a power reserved to each State to recall its delegates, or any of them, at any time within the year, and to send others in their stead for the remainder of the year.

No State shall be represented in Congress by less than two, nor more than seven members; and no person shall be capable of being a delegate for more than three years in any term of six years; nor shall any person, being a delegate, be capable of holding any office under the United States, for which he, or another for his benefit, receives any salary, fees or emolument of any kind.

Each State shall maintain its own delegates in a meeting of the States, and while they act as members of the committee of the States.

In determining questions in the United States in Congress assembled, each State shall have one vote.

Freedom of speech and debate in Congress shall not be impeached or questioned in any court or place out of Congress, and the members of Congress shall be protected in their persons from arrests or imprisonments, during the time of their going to and from, and attendence on Congress, except for treason, felony, or breach of the peace.

GLOSSARY

allegiance Loyalty.

boycott To refuse to buy a certain product.

confederation A union of states.

constituent A resident of a district represented by an elected official.

delegate A person who is authorized to represent another.

electoral college The body of electors chosen to elect the president and vice president of the United States.

garrison A military post.

judiciary A system of courts of law for the administration of justice.

legislature An organized body in charge of making laws.

mediate To resolve an issue by working with all the parties involved.

mercantilism A system of trade between colonies and their home nation.

militia A military force drawn from the civilian population.

monarchy A government by a ruler who usually reigns by heredity and for life.

mutiny Rebellion against authority.

nobility A class of high breeding and rank.

parliament A legislature or council where laws are made.

preamble An introductory statement that explains a document's purpose.

privateer A private ship taken over by the government in times of war.

ratify To approve.

reconciliation Reestablishing a close relationship.

repeal To take back.

treaty A formal agreement between two or more nations.

tyranny A government whose leader has absolute power over the people.

American Independence Museum
1 Governors Lane
Exeter, NH 03833
(603) 772-2622
Website: https://www.independencemuseum.org
Facebook: @americanindependencemuseum
The museum focuses on the events, people, places, and ideas that played a role in the nation's founding.

Canadian Museum of History
100 Laurier Street
Gatineau, QC, Canada K1A 0M8
(800) 555-5621
Website: http://www.historymuseum.ca
Facebook, Twitter, and Instagram: @CanMusHistory
The museum features an overview of Canadian immigration in the Crossroads of Culture collection.

Canadian War Museum
1 Vimy Place
Ottawa, ON, Canada K1A 0M8
(800) 555-5621
Website: http://www.warmuseum.ca
Facebook: @warmuseum
Twitter: @CanWarMuseum
Instagram: @canwarmuseum
This museum focuses on Canada's involvement in armed conflicts, including early wars in the country's history.

Independence National Historical Park
143 S. Third Street
Philadelphia, PA 19106
(215) 965-2305
Website: https://www.nps.gov/inde/index.htm

Facebook and Twitter: @indepdenceNHP
Instagram: @independencenps
The park's locations include the Liberty Bell Center, Independence Hall, Congress Hall, and more.

Library of Congress
101 Independence Avenue SE
Washington, DC 20540
(202) 707-5000
Website: http://www.loc.gov
Facebook: @libraryofcongress
Twitter and Instagram: @librarycongress
An ongoing exhibition at the Library of Congress features more than three thousand rare maps, documents, artifacts, and paintings on early America.

Museum of the American Revolution
101 S. Third Street
Philadelphia, PA 19106
(877) 740-1776
Email: info@amrevmuseum.org
Website: http://www.amrevmuseum.org
Facebook, Twitter, and Instagram: @amrevmuseum
This museum focuses on America's revolutionary beginnings.

Old Barracks Museum
101 Barrack Street
Trenton, NJ 08608
(609) 396-1776
Email: info@barracks.org
Website: http://www.barracks.org
Facebook and Instagram: @oldbarracksmuseum
Twitter: @theoldbarracks
This museum celebrates Colonial America with interpretive programs, exhibits, preservation, and more.

FOR FURTHER READING

Anderson, Marilyn. *Biographies of the American Revolution.* New York, NY: Rosen Publishing, 2013.

Davies, Monika. *True Life: Alexander Hamilton*. Huntington Beach, CA: Teacher Created Materials, 2017.

Hamilton, John. *American Revolution: The Road to War.* North Mankato, MN: Abdo Publishing, 2013.

Hamilton, John. *Final Years of the American Revolution.* North Mankato, MN: Abdo Publishing, 2013.

Hull, Mary E. *Witness the Boston Tea Party in United States History.* New York, NY: Enslow Publishing, 2015.

Lowery, Zoe. *The American Revolution.* New York, NY: Rosen Publishing, 2016.

Machajewski, Sarah. *Declaration of Independence.* New York, NY: Rosen Publishing, 2017.

Maloof, Torrey. *George Washington and the Men Who Shaped America*. Huntington Beach, CA: Teacher Created Materials, 2016.

Marciniak, Kristin. *The Revolutionary War: Why They Fought*. North Mankato, MN: Compass Point Books, 2015.

Perritano, John. *The Causes of the American Revolution.* New York, NY: Crabtree Publishing Company, 2013.

BIBLIOGRAPHY

Allison, Robert J., ed. *American Eras: Revolutionary Era, 1754–1783*. Detroit, MI: Gale, 1998.

"Bill of Rights (1791)." Our Documents. Retrieved March 4, 2018. https://www.ourdocuments.gov/doc.php?flash=false&doc=13.

Burnett, Edmund C., ed. *Letters of Members of the Continental Congress*. Gloucester, MA: P. Smith, 1963.

"Continental Congress to George Washington, June 19, 1775, Commission as Commander in Chief." George Washington Papers at the Library of Congress, 1741–1799: Series 8b, Manuscript Division. Library of Congress. http://edu.lva.virginia.gov/docs/GWCommission.pdf.

Greene, Jack, and J. R. Pole, eds. *The Blackwell Encyclopedia of the American Revolution*. Cambridge, MA: Blackwell, 1991.

Kukla, Jon. "Patrick Henry (1736–1799)." *Encyclopedia Virginia*, November 21, 2016. https://www.encyclopediavirginia.org/Henry_Patrick_1736-1799#start_entry.

"The Olive Branch Petition." Primary Sources Workshop in American History. Retrieved March 4, 2018. https://www.learner.org/workshops/primarysources/revolution/docs/olive.html.

Sanders, Jennings B. *Evolution of the Departments of the Continental Congress, 1774-1789.* Chapel Hill, NC: University of North Carolina Press, 1935.

Smith, Paul H. *Letters of Delegates to Congress, 1774–1789*. 26 vols. Washington, DC: Library of Congress, 1980.

Tourtellot, Arthur B. "... we mutually pledge to each other our Lives, our Fortunes, and our Sacred Honor." *American Heritage* 14, no. 1 (1962): 36–41.

INDEX

A

B

C

D

E

F

G

ABOUT THE AUTHORS

Xina M. Uhl discovered her love of history while still in grade school. She went on to obtain a master of arts in history from California State University, Northridge. After teaching college-level American history, she moved into educational writing. She has authored numerous nonfiction books for young people. When she is not writing or reading, she enjoys travel, photography, and hiking with her dogs. Her blog features book reviews, her travel adventures, and her latest fiction projects.

Betty Burnett is a Connecticut Yankee who grew up hearing stories of the Revolutionary War in New England. She is the author of multiple books of history and now lives in St. Louis, Missouri.

PHOTO CREDITS

Cover Architect of the Capitol; cover, p. 1 (flag) Piotr Krzeslak /Shutterstock.com; cover, p. 1 (scroll) Aleksandrs Bondars /Shutterstock.com; p. 3 Lone Wolf Photography/Shutterstock.com; pp. 4–5 (background) Enigmangels/Shutterstock.com; p. 5 (inset) courtesy of the University of Texas Libraries, The University of Texas at Austin; pp. 8, 15, 22, 28, 37, 45 (background) Zack Frank Shutterstock.com; p 9 MPI/Archive Photos/Getty Images; p. 10 Rare Book and Special Collections Division, Library of Congress; pp. 13, 20, 38 Manuscript Division. Library of Congress; p. 15 (inset) Lee Boltin/The LIFE Images Collection/Getty Images; p. 17 Attingham Park, Shropshire, UK/National Trust Photographic Library/John Hammond/Bridgeman Images; p. 23 Hulton Archive /Getty Images; p. 25 Karpeles Manuscript Library Museum; p. 27 Photo 12/Universal Images Group/Getty Images; p. 28 (inset) Fotosearch/Archive Photos/Getty Images; pp. 32, 33, 45 (inset) 47 National Archives and Records Administration; pp. 36, 49 © North Wind Picture Archives; p. 39 PHAS/Universal Images Group / Getty Images; p. 42 Reproduced from the original held by the Department of Special Collections of the Hesburgh Libraries of the University of Notre Dame Libraries.

Design: Michael Moy; Layout: Nicole Russo-Duca;
Photo Research: Nicole DiMella